Through a
Child's Eyes

Text & Photos by Donalyn Powell

Harold Shaw Publishers
Wheaton, Illinois

ISBN 0–87788–812–4

Library of Congress Cataloging-in-Publication Data

Powell, Donalyn.
    Through a child's eyes.

    1. Children—Prayer-books and devotions—English.
2. Children—Religious life.   I. Title.
BV4870.P63   1987   242'.62   87–4812
ISBN 0–87788–812–4

---

96 95 94 93 92 91 90 89 88 87

10 9 8 7 6 5 4 3 2 1

to the children

May you always fill our world
    with God's love
in trusting beauty and sparkling eyes.

Thank you, Lord, for this
gift of love from you—our unopened surprise package.
This unborn child is one of your loveliest
creative miracles.

Now help us, as parents, to be expressions
of your love.
Give us the
wisdom to direct this new life
in such a way
that our child may grow into a
light in the world for you.

____

Then he placed a little child among them; and taking the child in his arms he said to them, "Anyone who welcomes a little child like this in my name is welcoming me, and anyone who welcomes me is welcoming my Father who sent me!"

Mark 9:36–37 TLB

I have this friend.

We play together,

share together,

laugh together,

   and

together we feel

God's joy in us.

"**...L**et us practice loving each other,

for love comes from God

and those who are loving and kind

show that they are the children of God,

and that they are

getting to know him better."

1 John 4:7 TLB

Do you think God
made this dirt road
for us to play on?

Sure he did!

Well, then, why does
Mama get mad
when we come home
so muddy?

"Seek, and you will find . . ."

Matthew 7:7b TLB

If we could only

handle our mistakes

the same way we play

with dandelions—

pick them up,

learn from them,

and blow them away!

"... Anyone who humbles himself

as this little child

is the greatest

in the Kingdom of heaven."

Matthew 18:4 TLB

The joy of touch—

the softness of fur,

the roughness of stones,

the silk of flowers,

the wetness of water . . .

Gifts don't always

have a price tag.

When God gives presents

they are so generous that

we can share them

and still have them.

Even in
a crowd,
a child is always
special.

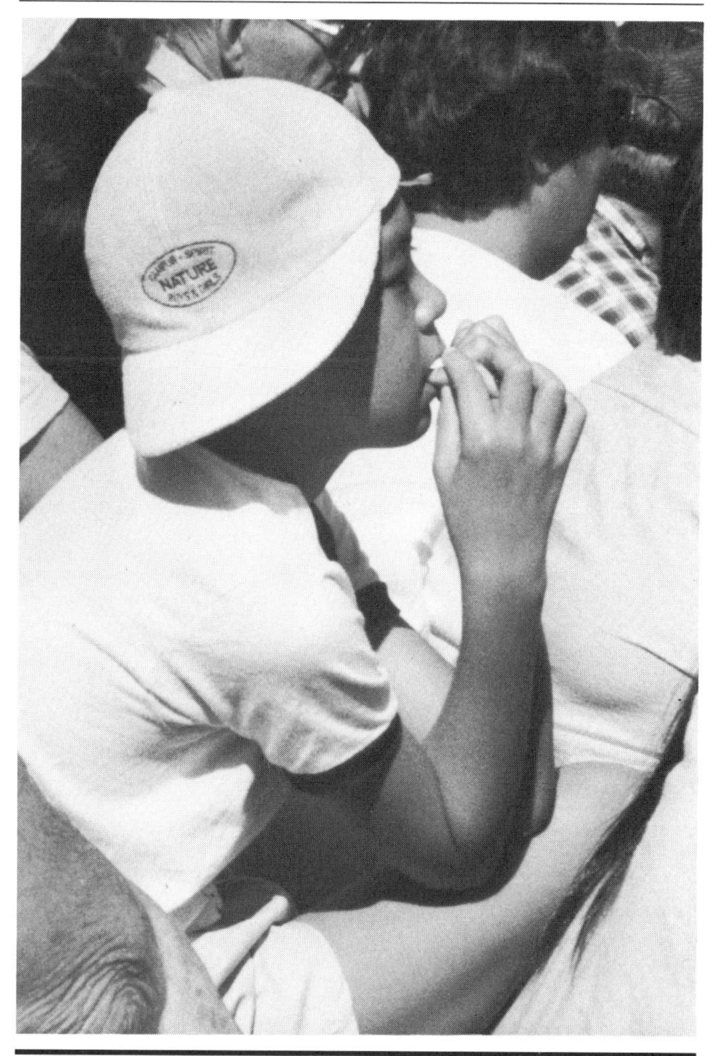
NATURE

Some secret things are hard to find,

but when we keep at it

it's always worth it.

Loving God is easy.

Following God isn't

always easy, but

when we keep at it

it's always worth it.

Love is sometimes

easier felt

than spoken . . .

____

"**A**nd the streets

will be filled

with boys and girls

at play."

Zechariah 8:5 *TLB*

Everybody's been looking

for Jesus, and he's been

here all along.

All you have to do is

sit quiet enough

to hear him.

Every child

has a special gleam

like no one else.

If we could only

see the world fresh—

through a child's eyes . . .

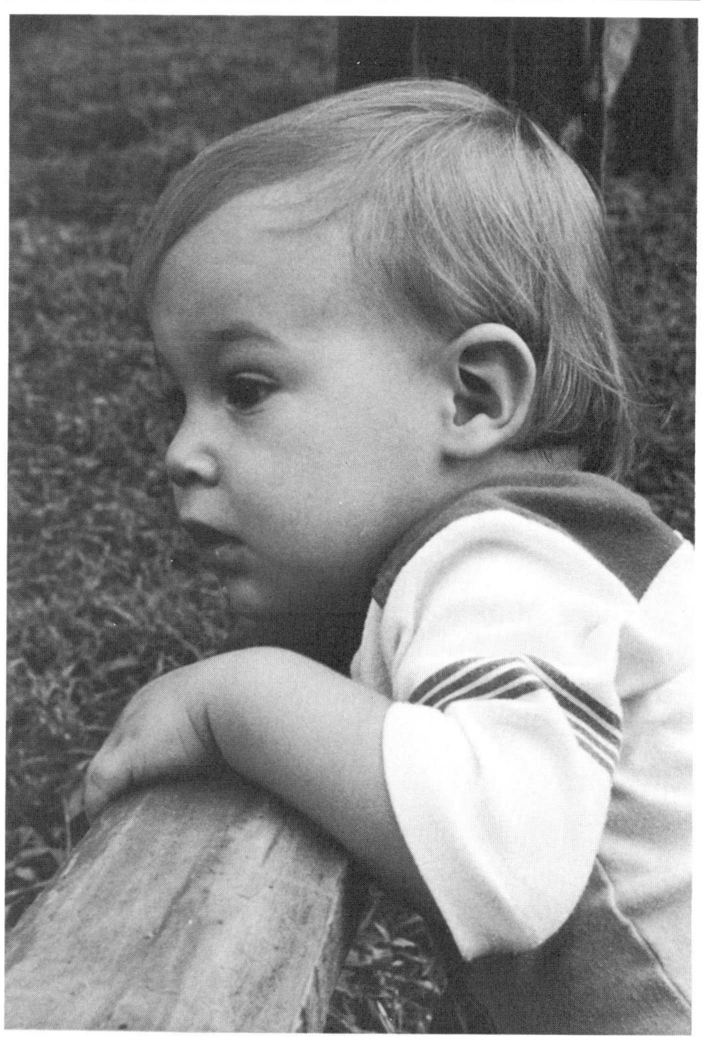

Thank you, Jesus,

for all the fun

we had today.

I don't know what

we're doing tomorrow,

but you already

know that anyway.

At the end of the day, something is
always left behind . . .

A smile,

A hug,

A giggle,

A blessing—

and tennis shoes.

Through your eyes—add your own

favorite photos,

shower sentiments,

birth announcements,

memories of growing-up,

and dreams for the future.